# O.C.D

## LIVING WITH OBSESSION AS PASSION

PAVAN SHARMA

Dedicate My Book....

O.C.D Is my First Novel/book

ever to be published as a Writer,

So i will dedicate this book

to 'only and only' to my

Father Mr. Purendra Kumar Sharma

And My Mother Mr's. Usha Priyadarshini Sharma

# Contents

A Litte brief about my Parent's...
My Father dream't of,
becoming a successful director,
at a very young age....
So Eventually he got A "National Award"
as a Producer for his First...Punjabi Film
on Family Planning..
"Kade Dhup Kade Chavn" in 1969.
And he also had many more prestigious
T.V show's to his credit's....

My Mother was also a Producer,
And she is probably the only Producer..
In the whole world to Produce A Serial
On "Martial Art's".......(13 episodes)

# Preface

'OCD'

    Obsessive Compulsive Disorder..
    Today's world is dealing with one or the other Obsession's.
    Specially post Pandemic,
    It has become every household's topic.
    Obssesion could be of a
    Love,shopping,eating,laughing
    Drinking,Smoking, Driving,
    being on social media all the time's,
    And Washing Hand's etc....

OCD my this novel/ story revolve's around
    Our Hero Ashutosh Singh...
    He's being Obsessed of washing hand's..
    He washe's hand's some 50 to 60 time's a day.
    And He hide's this habbit of his from the outside world.
    But eventually how he meet's a Female Counsellor
    And She take's him to his past life,
    And from there what happen's
    That's the story 'OCD' is all about...

# ONE

## OCD

Obssesive Compulsive disorder.
   As my film title suggest
   the film is about OCD.


ASHUTOSH SINGH ( Hero )
   His Character Sketch...
   Our story Hero Ashutosh Singh who is fondly known as,
   Ashu by his family and very close friend's.
   He is a bachelor...
   He is doing his Post graduation in Advertising.
   He live's with His Father Satish Singh
   And Mother Sunaina Singh..
   He is the only son...
   His father is probably the richest man In town,
   Who own's marketing advertising firm,
   For which Ashutosh is pursuing his advertising degree,
   and he want's to follow his father's footstep.
   And That is his dream....
   Ashutosh is today's man around 26-27 of age.
   He play's all sport's he dance's like a Pro.
   So in short he is the dream man for every girl In this town.
   On the Other hand...
   SARAH BISHT ( Female Lead)
   Sarah Bisht, the female lead age 22+24
   She is an Orphan.
   She is studying for her doctor degree as a

Counsellor/Psychiatrist in scholarship....
She is extremely Beautiful,
She has big fan following in the University,
Not only because of her look's,
but also With her academic's.
She is amazing dancer,
She dance's in India Kathak fusion Mix form,
and she has won load's of trophie's,
Not only for herself but also for her University..
She is single, a loner, but very expressive at time's,
She is looking for her dream boy.....

Story.....

# TWO
## CHAPTER 1

So the story open's from the event which is gonna take place.
It's an huge University with all the facultie's of every subject's.
It's Some where in Madhya Pardesh(India)
Today Ashutosh and Sarah along with many other student's
Are about to perform their dance performance's.
As it is the Final day for final year student's..
Since Ashutosh is in final year,
so it is his last year in the university....

Interior University Auditorium....
Day time....11.30 AM

The story open's with Principle annoucing on the stage..

Principle: so student's as we all know..
this year will be the last year for our final year student's.
Some will become a doctor some engineer's some in sport's,
and some in advertising feild's...
Fashion ,sport's blah blah blah....
As it will be the last year for some student's,
So we the University teacher's
Has made it extra special for all of us.
We will have a competion,
between the final year student's and the junior's.
(Student's applause they start cheering).
Principle: apney hon haar birvaan key hoth chikney path..

(Bright student's have rough path's)...
(Student's laugh's..)
Prncy: So get ready for extra fun.
(Student's cheer's again)
Princy: today who will start this event any guesses??
Student's:: who else sir!!
Ashu Ashu Ashu....
( And all student's start shouting Ashu's name)
Princy: yes you all are right.. its is our own hero...
The charismatic,generous good looker,very good in sport's
brilliant student, always topper
hamarey colleage ki aan baan aur shaan
( Pride of our university)
Hamara Ashutosh Singh.
( Our own Ashutosh)...
(Student's clap's cheering Ashu Ashu)..
All of a sudden a big bang happen's.
It become's a pin drop silence....
All the student's await's for Ashu's entry...
We show his shoes following on the stage.
He spin's around and stop's....
So from his feet's to his body to his face
camera goes up and ....
Slowly slowly in slow motion his face is revealed.
(Tight close of Ashu).
Student's start whistling clapping shouting,
Ashu Ashu ( whistle's)
So lighter beat's start's then louder
and full song start's playing...
Ashutosh is dancing like a the man for the day...
Music end's Ashu is smiling acknowledging his fellow student's.


One student on micc ruchi: so friend's this was our own Ashu,
    Let's hear it for him..
    ( Everybody clap's and whistle's).
    Ruchi on micc: so our next performer is 2'nd year student Miss kala..
    Kala recite's a poem same time the camera is going in the changing room,
    As the camera enter's the changing room

there are alot of girl's getting ready.

For there performance's,

Ruchi announce's: so our next group performance is by savy and her wing's

So welcome them on stage.

All the girl's come running on stage and some catchy musical dance happen's

(In the changing room Avantika say's)

Avantika: commo'n Sarah hurry up next is your performance dear.

Avantika tie's her blouse from back.

(We show Sarah is applying lip gloss then a mascara and a small bindi, but we have not revealed her face yet.)

Ruchi on stage: so next and also the last performance is

any guesses guyss????

Student from crowd; Apni Sarah( our own Sarah)

Ruchi: yes you are right it is Sarah Bisht..

(Student's start's shouting her name Sarah Sarah)....

Sarah start's walking toward's the stage.

Ashu is also standing waiting for her.

Probably he has not seen her yet....

We show Sarah back walking,

(She reache's toward's the stage bend's down to offer the prayer's.

As she get's up)

Someone from crowd: there she is. Sarah...

Ruchi: so here we are with our last performance,

Aapki apni sabki Sarah bisht.... ( Your own Saara Bisht)

Student's clap's...

Now it's just pin drop silence.

Sarah face is stil not revealed yet.

Ashu to trying to take one glimp of her...

But couldn't succeed...

Now the Music start's...

a music piece of ghungroo.

Sarah get's her feet's on the stage...

As Tabla plays Sarah come's on the stage with her back facing the student's.

Some student's: arey face dikha do Sarah ji. ( Show your face Sarah)

While Music play's Sarah with her hand's says wait don't be in a hurry..

So it's ghungroo tabla sitar mix she dance's without revealing her face, and big bang happen's she turn's around and the spot light goes on her face.

She is standing in kathak mudra....

Ashu see's Sarah for the first time and he is mesmerized...

Student's in the crowd: aye haye ( simple wow)....

Sarah smile's and then a mixture of indian western music play's.

Sarah dance's in fusion indian western hip hop mix.

And the music come's to an end...

She stand's there in her last mudra.

Everybody is stuned complete pin drop silence,

Ashu is also jaw drop....

Then Ashu start's clapping so does the entire auditorium,

So now auditorium is surrounded by clapping whistling noise

Student's start's shouting Sarah Sarah....

Judge's too are confused whom to declare 1$^{st}$ and 2$^{nd}$

Principle walk's on the stage while saying...

Princy: so we witnessed some extra ordinary performance's today,

Everyone who performed were absolutely amazing.

But the one's who are best will be the winner's today.

any idea who is the winner student's???

( he ask's student's)

Student: Sarah

other say's: no Ashu

Half the side shout's Sarah and half the side say's Ashu..

Principle; exactly along with the judge's we all are also confused

That who is number 1 and 2..

But for me both are the winner's..

But one has to loose and another is the winner.

So the second prize goes to goes to Ashu.....

Ashu smile's and agree's: yes i agree that Sarah was awesome.

Priciple gives Ashu a smaller cup.

Student's clap's.....

And Princy anounce's

Princy: so this year winner is none other than Sarah.

Sarah is exstatic. Student's are in joy.. ribbon's start's to drop from everywhere,

Whistling and clapping happen's

Everybody start's shouting Sarah Sarah...

Princy: hand's over the winner trophy to Sarah.
    hey both of you are our universities best student's.
    Enjoy guyss...
    (Sarah Ashu shake's hand's)..
    They both meet for the first time...
    Sarah introduces herself
    Sarah:: hi nice to meet you.
    Ashutosh: likewise congratulation's..
    Sarah: thank you so much...
    Both are Very happy to meet each other...
    Student's are cheering! Ashu Sarah..
    .Sarah takes the micc and anounce's on the stage that
    Sarah: since this is last year for our senior's
    Just like Ashutosh and other fellow student's
    We as junior's have thrown a party for our senior's..
    Its a good luck farewell party in the university activity center,
    So everyone is invited today in the evening.
    Student's start's cheering: yeah yeah they clap and whistle's

# THREE

## CHAPTER 2

Evening interior of Activity Center...

Everybody reaches to the Venue...
Music is playing there is a mini bar counter which is open..
Every student and teacher's are dressed up smartly for the party tonight
Ashu has already reached.
He is having good time's with his friend's.
He is showing all the card trick's and looking at the watch again and again,
He is looking dapper... His eye's are searching for Sarah,
All of a sudden music stop's...
As the spotlight reaches to the main door
We show Sarah is standing...
She's is wearing amazing western dress...
she's looking ravishing stunning,
Beautiful like a barbie doll....
Ashutosh see her he couldn't able to keep his eye's away,
and all of a sudden he reache's to Sarah,
He Gives his hand to Sarah,
Sarah with a big smile give's her hand too,
Ashu pull's Sarah on stage and...
The Music start's playing....
with jazz salsa American Latin fusion mix.
They both dances Tango( Latin dance)...
They dance like a Couple made for each other.
For three minutes it is just music Ashu and Sarah dances..

Everyone standing there are just witnessing..
A beautiful couple dance.
As Music end's its pin drop silence...
Sarah Ashutosh Looking at each other in each other's arm's.
They are looking each other's eye to eye like one soul.
Its pin drop silence. All the student's are frozen.
Ashu smile's looking at Sarah.
Sarah to response with a big smile,
Someone from the crowd scream's
Woooow,
As Student's notice's this they start clapping.
Student's starts cheering,
Ashu Sarah Ashu Sarah
Now Ashu Sarah both realise this...
And they both get back to their self's.
Everybody surround's them and start shouting
Sara Ashu...Ashu Sara...Sara Ashu...
Ashu and Sarah acknowledge the student's.
They both bow down in appreciation.
All of a sudden some guy come's from the crowd,
He comes toward's Sarah ask's...Sarah!
Boy: lets leave Sarah as we getting late,
Pull's Sarah and take her away.
Seeing this Ashutosh get's awkward
Ashu Goes toward's the bar counter and
takes 3 4 shot's...pick's his bike key's and his jacket
And leave's the auditorium....
Sarah ask's...
Sarah: what happen to him,why did he leave?
Her best friend Avantika say's...
Avantika: dont you know that....
The entire unversity know's Ashutosh has never approached,
any girl ever before, and today we all were shocked!
he danced with you,
I think he like's you.
But i guess Seeing Yash may be he think's ...
That Yash is your boyfriend.....
Sarah reaction is like What!??...

# FOUR

## CHAPTER 3

Exterior Ashu's house

Night...

Ashutosh reache's his house.

Park's his bike and press the door bell.

his mother Sunaina open's the door...

Sunaina middle aged very beautiful poised and elegant lady

She open's the door and ask's...

Sunaina: Hey my son..you are back..

So how was your evening Son..

Ashu greet's her,

Ashu: hii Mom...evening ok ok Mom,

Father is also sitting in the living room.

Satish Singh he is around 55 year's,

Very atractive handsome personality of his age

Smoking a pipe...

Satish notice's something Say's...

Satish: it seems bad evening Son,

Ashu: hi Dad...

And he goes up to his room.

Sunaina ask's Satish in sign language...

( What happened).

Satish replies in sign language

Dont know...

Satish: Ashu will you have dinner??

Ashu from upstair's

Ashu: no dad i had it.

Satish: ( whisper's) must be tired.
Sunaina: ya it seem's like...
Ashu throw's his bike key's, remove his shoe's and
Fall's down on the bed....
And start visualising the evening,
and start Whispering...
Ashu: "What Sara why do you have a boy friend".
Suddenly the door bell ring's...
Sunaina open's the door and find's a beautiful girl standing
It's Sarah...
Sarah: hello Aunty is Ashutosh home??
Sunaina: yes he's just came.
Sarah introduce's herself ...
Sarah: i am Sarah from Ashutosh's unversity,
can i meet him for a minute
Sunaina say's...
Ashu your friend has come.
Ashu say's...
Ashu: yes Mom coming....
As He come's down and he Find's Sarah standing....
Ashu is shocked to see her..
Sarah: hi
Ashu: hello but how come???
Sunaina ask's Sarah to come in
Sarah say's....
Sarah: i will love to visit again auntyji.
I just need to speak with Ashutosh for a minute.
Ashu pick's his jacket and pick's his bike key's...
and Ashu step's out...
Satish Ashu' father say's...
Satish: I think it's good evening now for Ashu...
Sunaina Satish both smile's..
Ashu look at the car where
Yash is standing..
he's the same guy who came up to Sarah on the dance floor,
Ashu ask's...
Ashu : " so why are you here."
Sarah hold's Ashu's hand and walk toward's the car.

Yash say's...
Yash: buddy Sarah is my best friend,
but i have my girlfriend( point's toward's the car)
Avantika Who was sitting in the car."
Avantika say's "hi Ashu.
Sarah is single and i think
She like's you."...Alot
Sarah say's.. idiot you embarassed me.
Avantika: what embarrased. Since you left Ashu
Sarah Is constanty asking.
Why did you leave. Why did he leave...
I have to meet him. So mam here is Ashu
Ashu this is Sarah. Happy Family,
They all laugh...
Yash say's ..guy's we were heading
For night out i think..
You guy's need some time together,
Avantika: yes i think, we will leave...
So Sarah i will call and i will pick you.
Ashu say's ...
Ashu: dont worry i will drop her.
Avantika yash : ok sure and they leave's
Byeee guy's.
Sarah: byeee.
Now Ashu Sarah start's Walking...
Its full blue moon...
Sky is as clear as water...
Star twinkling...
It Feel's like Romance is in full swing...
They both are walking...
looking at each other and smiling.
"So you are a doctor huh. Ashu asks!
"Sarah nodes her head...
Sarah: "yes."
"And you are into Advertising huh."
"Sarah Ask's
Ashu say's : "yes"
Ashu : thats my father's dream (he say's)

To be the number one advertising guy...
In this whole world.
Sarah say's: yes i met your parent's they were very nice
And very humble....
Sarah: "I miss my parent's." She say's
Ashu: So what.. you can call them now,
and speak with them....
(Ashu take's out his phone and ask's for their number)....
Sarah look's down replies.
Sarah: I don't have my family by birth.
I am orphan studying on scholarship...
(Ashu realise's that Sarah has become sad
so he tries to cheer her up)
He say's jokingly...
Ashu: no no you are not alone now ....
You Have a family.. your boy friend and his parent's..
Sarah ask's...
Sarah: is it and who is my boy friend?
Ashu say's
"Me."!!
Sarah look's at him they both look at each.
Ashu goes down on his knee's,
He could not find anything,
So he pick's up a stone
And....
He's Gesturing as if he's holding a flower,
and Ashu say's:
Ashu: With the Swear Of God...
blue moon... Sky... Star's...
and and and.....
He look's around..couldn't see any flower
Say's:
Ashu: even this stone i take you as my
Beloved girl friend...happily ever after..
After seeing this Sarah burst's out laughing...
Sarah say's
"you are mad."
Ashu say's ....NO! now i am not...

Sarah ask's... what do you mean?
By saying... now you are not?..
Ashu say's: before people use to say that.....
Now i think i am not Mad anymore...
Sarah burst out laughing even louder..
Suddenly Sarah notices...
Ashu's your shoe lace was open..
Sarah: hey Ashu your shoe lace is open.
Ashu notices ....
Ashu: yes you right i will tie it later...
She say's....
Sarah: Dear you will fall down... Please tie it...
Ashu: No... i wont ...i will do it later
Ashu say's
"Please you tie it up." Sarah say's...
Repeated refusals of Ashu
Sarah notices Ashu's behaviour
Before She say's it again...
Ashu: hey i am hungry will have you dinner with me.
Sarah: ok but......
Ashu run's toward's his bike.
Sarah: loudly she says: atleast tie your shoe lace,
Ashu: while running ( yes i will).
Ashu take's out his bike and come's toward's Sarah.
Ashu : your driver at your service Mam.
Be the first lady to sit behind me on my bike.
Sarah smile's and sit's behind Ashu.
And he ride's toward's some restaurant.
He come's and park his bike at a chinese restuarant.
Ashu: chinese will do.
Sarah: yes i love chinese.
Ashu: let's go in.

# FIVE

## CHAPTER 4

Interior of Tick Tock chinese restaurant.

It seem's Ashu and his parent's are regular visitor there.
   Because as he entered from the gate keeper to the staff
   Everyone know's Ashu.
   (They both reach to one corner.
   Probably Ashu's favourite Table).
   Sarah: it seem's you come here quite often.??
   Ashu: yes you are right. Me and my parent's visit's here every week
   (As they both were talking),
   the stewert come's his name is rahul,
   Rahul: good evening Ashu Sir.
   Ashu: hey buddy.
   Rahul: good evening mam
   Sarah smile's at him.
   Rahul: so sir here is the Menu.
   Rahul give's menu to both of them...
   Ashu: buddy my is usual my favourite
   Chicken hakka noodles.
   Sarah: i will too have the same please.
   (While rahul is placing the order.
   he notice's Ashu shoe lace was open)
   Rahul: Ashu sir your shoe lace is open.
   Ashu: arey bhai. Yes it's new fashion.
   (and makes a gesture to Rahul to please go.
   Rahul leave's).

While Ashu is about to speak with Sarah.
A knife which was kept on the table fall's down,
(Sarah notices it but potray's as if she is reading the menu.
Ashu think's Sarah did not notice that)..
(So to pick up the knife is a big deal for Ashu.
Then he realises that he will pick up the knife and the same time,
he will tie his shoe lace and after which he can wash his hand's.)
So he think's Sarah is not noticing.
Slowly slowly he goes down ,
tie his shoe lace and he pick's up the knife.
Sarah has noticed everything..
Ashu: hey i just come i need to go to the wahroom.
Sarah: ok sure....
Ashu leave's towards the sink.. Sarah follow's him.
She hide's behind the wall,
And she start noticing Ashu's mannerism...
Ashu look's around doesn't find's anyone.
So he start's washing his hand's....
He washes one time. Then he washes again.
Sarah see's all this...
Ashu washes again and fourth and then the fifth time.
As he is about to turn he stop's ,
and washes his hand's again for 5 more time's.
Sarah see's all this and,
She realise's that Ashu has OCD Of washing hand's.
Sarah goes back to the table and settle's down.
Ashu come's back. As they both come back.
Rahut too get's the dinner.
Rahul: here you are Ashu Sir and Mam.
Rahul serve's the food and leaves. (Ashu smile's)
Ashu: so??
Sarah...so??? What!
Ashu: while eating.. how's the food??
Sarah: really nice.. ( while eating she say's)
Sarah: can i ask you a Question??
Ashu: yes sure!!
Sarah: since when you have this.??
Ashu: my love for you?? (Smiles)

Ashu: the moment i saw you for the first time..
Sarah: (laughs)no what i mean is you are OCD.... Right! ??
Ashu says : OCD.. he get's offended but does not show's that,
He pretend's not to know much about that.
Ashu: what is OCD???
Sarah: Ashu i am your wel-wisher. I really like you,
And i care about you. .
OCD is quite normal nowaday's.
And sorry to say.. after you did not tie your shoe lace,
You got my attention.. see i am psychiatrist.
I read about OCD everyday ...
Sarah: if you want to share with me it will be fine with me.
She keep's her hand on Ashu' s hand.
Sarah: trust me you can talk about it.
Ashu: ( who was offended now get's a little comfertable for talking about it),

Ashu: ok besides my parent's
You will be the first person whom i will be sharing my secret.
Sarah: it is my honour Ashu. I care for you ,
Ashu: ( smiles) yes i have OCD.
And i also know it can be cured but i am scared.
Sarah: don't be afraid. I am with you,
Ashu: Ya ya i know you are a counsellor..
So why don't you take up my case.
Sarah: yes i am already working on it.
Ashu: so what will be done??
Will i be sent to some rehab or something??
Sarah: no not atall..
Ashu: really.. then some medicines??
Sarah: may be later if needed.
Ashu: huh no rehab no medicine's then how??
Sarah: a simple process is by pactising ,
taking you in your past life with
Past life Regression...
Ashu: means ??
Sarah: i will take you at that same period
or you can say that same time,
when you developed this obsession.

It is by taking you back in your past life..
Ashu: what you will take me back in my past life.
Sarah: yes..
Ashu: seriously. This is sounding so cool.
Mam please take me back in my past life.
Sarah: ok i will may be tommorow.
Ashu: no tommorow tonight..
And call's rahul..
Sarah: arey Ashu wait a minute.
Ashu: nop...
Rahul comes with the bill's.
Ashu pay's the bill's and they both leave's..

Exterior of the restaurant...
Ashu start's his bike and they both reaches to Sarah hostel.

Sarah hostel midnight...
Exterior...

# **SIX**
## CHAPTER 5

Ashu: so mam let's go inside your house..
Sarah: smile's you are very rigid..
Ashu: yes very. Mam i have loved you so it's with full honesty,
Sarah smile's.. they both laugh's as they enter's Sarah clinic.

Sarah's clinic
Interior...
Sarah switch on the light's...
Ashu look's around.
He find's a hostel kind of studio apartment.
And also he see's a big huge desk top.
As he turn's around find's Sarah is already
Wearing Doctor's Coat and she is holding a stethoscope,
Sarah: come here Ashu. And she show's him on the desk top.
Ashu: you look cute in the Coat.
( He is trying to be little romantic).
Sarah: Mr. Ashu. Please be little serious.
Ashu: (laugh's) ok ok mam.
Sarah show's the graphics on the desk top.
She show's Ashu the whole procedure.
Sarah tell's him ...
"Ashu stay calm and stay relaxed.
Ashu: yes i am relaxed..
Then Sarah check's Ashu's pulse.
Sarah: pulse is normal. Perfect. Let me check your
Eyes.

Ashu come's closer.
Sarah: it's looking fine...so everything seem's perfect.
Ashu: yes mam.
Sarah: before i start i need to ask you some very important question's.
Ashu: ok please ask.
Sarah: do you know exactly when had you developed this OCD.
Ashu: yes i remmember. It was Diwali that night. I think i was
7 year's then. I bursted some cracker's.
So one rocket went in our neighbour's house.
Sarah: smile's.
Ashu: after which we went to our farm house
we were sleeping...
and in my Dream's...
i saw a murder of a lady and a boy of 7 year's.
Sarah: then???
Ashu: i screamed and i got up,
Mom and Dad came running to my room.
I went unconscious.
So when i came to my conscious it was after 15 day's.
According to my parent's i was critical...
It took 15 day's for me to recover...
Ashu: then i don't even came to know,
slowly and gradualy this washing hand's started.
Sarah: ok ok. No problem. So we will try to reach this point of your age.
And you don't worry just keep following my instruction's"
Shall we start...
Ashu: yes mam.. let's do it.
Sarah make's him sit in a very comfortable chair.
Now Sarah start's the process of taking Ashu to his past life
Now as he's going through the journey..
Sarah ask's him..
Sarah: so we are entering the process,
She ask's: what happened 10 minute's back?
Ashu say's...i was telling you about that night.

Tell me Sarah ask's what happened... 30 minutes back
Ashu say's.... we both were in the resturant.
I went to wash hand's

And you were spying on me.(he smile's).
Sarah to smile's....
What happened 2 hours back Sarah ask's....
Ashu say's we were dancing Tango.
What happened 10 day's back she ask's..
Now ashu is going deeper in his unconscious mind,
And the journey is going through.
As he stop's traveling in time zone,
Ashu say's: i was playing football.
I kicked the ball which went on to hit
Sangram Sir our Sport's teacher
Ball hit's his head and his Wig came off ,
Everybody in the campus were laughing at him.
Sarah: gigle's....
So she keep asking about certain year's
And they reach a point where Ashu is 17...
Sarah: Ashu please concentrate...
what happened when you were 17.??
Any big event if happened then?
Ashu:: yes Dad (Satish his father)
gifted me a sport's bike the same bike
on which we both came to your clinic,
I took Dad and Mom for a ride.
So much fun we three had.
Sarah: ok Ashu concentrate even deeper ,
so we are entering the same point,
Whcn you were At the age of 7...
So What happened then.
Ashu start concentrating..
Sarah is writting everything on a paper.
Ashu is getting restless his body start's reacting agressively
He see's a train.
Ashu: i see a train
Sarah: ok
Ashu: now i can see a station there is name plate
But i think the whole name is not visible.
It seem's there are sticker's stuck over plate.
But but i can see it is in yellow color,

And the last alphabet is capital M..
Sarah note's it down.
Ashu :continuous.
i see a station master holding green flag.
Sarah: ok..
Ashu: now i see it's lightening. It seems it's gonna rain.
Sarah notes it down.
Sarah: then!!!
Ashu say's: i can see a farm house.
Its written Ranjit Thakur Number 603.
Now he adds further. I can see a out of focus farm house.
Now i see a bedroom.
I see a lady is running after a small boy.
Boy is running and he come's to the stair Case..
Lady too come's running behind him...
Ashu states all of a sudden someone pushed the lady
she fall's from the stair's.
Ashu is getting restless now.
He add's: Someone pushed the boy too.
Both are on the floor,
Lady is saying something...
Lady: Ranjit leaves us please leave my son.
You take everything you want.
Out of focus. A man speak's
i cannot see anyone one Ashu Say's
Man: i told you but you were not listening.
Now because of you the boy will also Die..
Lady: no please leave my son. Noooo,
Now man hand is revealed. He's holding a pistol.
He shoot's the lady...
Ashu get's scared shout's...
Ashu: lady got killed lady got killed.
He will kill the boy he will kill the boy.
As that man is about to kill the boy.
Out of focus a lady scream's..
listening to the Scream even Ashu get's up
Screaming!???
Ashu is scared and,

He get's up with a loud Scream.
Ashu: lady got killed got killed.
Ashu is all perspering. His pulse is running very fast,
Seeing this Sarah to get's scared. She hold's Ashu.
Sarah: Ashu calm down. She trie's to calm Ashu down.
Ashu has lost so much energy that he get unconcious and he fall's asleep.
Sarah. Hold's Ashu closer make's him sleep on the floor on the matress.
And she too lay's down with him.
Looking at him Ashu is sleeping
Sarah too fall's asleep.

# SEVEN

## CHAPTER 6

Next day morning its 7.30 AM.

Sarah open's the curtain's... Look's at Ashu.

Ashu get's up he slowly open's his eyes

Look's at Sarah...

Sarah come's..Good morning..

bed tea is ready... Sir (she smile's)

Ashu: good morning....

Ok let me fresh and up.. say's Ashu

Sarah: ok sir.. Ashu your Mom was calling,

I spoke with her in the Morning,

Call her and speak with her...

She was asking for you Sarah say's

Ashu : ok i will.

Ashu come's back sit's on the chair

Sarah: so boss how are you feeling today.

Ashu: good mam. Who were they.

Sarah: must be some connection's with your past.

As Sarah speak's and the phone ring's

Sunaina is calling...

Ashu pick's up the phone and speak's with Sunaina,

Sunaina says..

So finally my Son has found his girlfriend..

Ashu smile's..nothing like that Mom.

Sunaina say's : come home and

Get Sarah Along for lunch.

Ashu: let me ask Sarah

Whisper's he ask's Sarah.
Ashu: Mom's calling us for lunch.
Sarah realise the last night situation she say's
Sarah: yes we will go for lunch.
Ashu: ok Mom we be there....

# EIGHT
## CHAPTER 7

Ashu's house exterior day time...

Ashu park's his bike.
    Sarah and Ashu reache's home for lunch.
    Ashu presses the door bell.
    Sunaina open's the door.
    Sunaina: hello my son.
    Welcome home,
    Ashu smile's: what Mom anything!
    And they both smile's.
    Sunaina greet's Sarah...
    Sunaina: welcome dear.
    Sarah: thank you so much Auntyji.
    Satish: welcome my Son... Hi Sarah..
    Sarah : hello uncle.
    Ashu settle's down so does Sarah.
    Sunaina start's to arrange the table for lunch,
    Sarah: let me help you auntyji.
    Satish to Ashu: nice choice buddy( wink's)
    Ashu: dad we are just friend's. But i think i like her.
    Satish: and what about Sarah? She likes you.?
    Ashu: yes i think so.
    Sunaina: Sarah Ashu is just like a kid. He want's food on time.
    Sarah: yes auntyji he took me to your favourite restaurant.
    Last night...
    Sunaina: oh really.

Sarah: so i saw he has quite good diet. Touch wood.

Sunaina smile's

So they all are having lunch together....

While having lunch Sunaina Satish tell all

Funny incident's about Ashu.

Sunaina: Sarah when he was very young

he was bursting cracker's

Sarah cut's in between:

Sarah: yes and one rocket went inside your neighbour's house.

Sunaina: wow my son's first date with Sarah

And she know's everything.

Now teasing Sunaina adds on...

Sunaina: when Ashu was 17

on his birthday his father gifted him,

Again Sarah cut's Sunaina in between,

Sarah: uncle gifted Ashu his sport's bike.

Satish: (mischiviously) i am impressed Son you have told everything to Sarah.

Ashu: feel's embarrased so does Sarah...

Satish : so Son please let us know,

when are you both getting married.

Ashu: that we will after exam's.

Not realising Satish was pulling his leg's

Ashu: what!!!

They all burst out laughing.

Sunaina: come Sarah let me show you,

Some of Ashu's childhood pics...

She show's the pic's when he played a king in one of school's event.

Sarah admires the pic's... Sunaina keep swaping the page's

This is that day when Satish gifted him the bike.

Now she show's that pic in which he bursted the cracker's.

As Sarah See's that pic of Ashu and his parent's standing at the farm house.

Glass filled with water slip's of Ashu's hand's.

Sarah: oho let me get the cloth. She goes in the kitchen to get the cloth,

Sunaina close's the album...

Sarah bring's the cloth. Wipe all the water on the table.

Ashu: lovingly say's: thank you.

Sarah: exchanging look's. No issues.(Smiles)
After keeping the glass in the kitchen Sarah ask's Ashu
Sarah: shall we leave. It's evening now..
Satish: yes son drop her.
Sunaina: it was wonderful meeting you,
Keep coming Sarah. This is your own house now,
Sarah: i loved meeting you both Auntyji.
Yes i wil meet you both quite often now.
Sarah: bye auntyji bye uncle.
Satish/Sunaina: bye beta...
Ashu and Sarah leave's.
( Exterior Ashu house day)
Sunaina: they both look's great together.
Satish: yes indeed( they both smiles).
Ashu Is riding his bike very quitely..
Remembering what happened last night,
As they reach to Sarah's hostel...

# NINE

## CHAPTER 8

(Sarah's clinic's exterior day time say 5.30PM)
 Ashu stop's his bike ask's: who were they.
 Sara say's... dont worry dear...
 It must be related to your life in past.
 So don't worry.... We wil find it out,
 Ashu ask's: it was my past life???
 Sarah: yes!!
 Ashu : I want see that again.
 Sara say's ...no not now let this sink In you.
 Ashu insist's alot...please please!!
 i want to know what happened.
 By now Sarah has known about Ashu's nature.
 Now she know's Ashu is Very rigid.
 So they......reach to her clinic again..

Sarah' s clinic ( inside its 6 PM).

(Sun is settling down it's becoming little darker)
 Sara say's: Ashu you promise me what'ever happen's ..
 You will not Get up immediately....
 Just relax.. i am here,
 (She hold's his Hand...)..
 Sarah: Are you ok! shall we start.???
 Ashu: yes we should...
 (So the same process begin's again.)..
 And now Ashu reache's to his past life,

where Once again he see his past life but...
he's is trying his level best,
but he couldn't see anything..
Sarah; what do you see Ashu?
Ashu: nothing.. i see nothing atall.
(Sarah understand's...
that Ashu has taken alot of tension and,
this process need's relaxed mind.)
So she trie's one more time..
Sarah: just focus Ashu.
Let us try again one more time...
(Ashu is trying really hard but it's of no use.
He is not able to see anything.)
Ashu: i cannot see anything.
(now he's getting restless)
Sarah: read's the situation.
Ashu slowly open your eye's she say's...
Ashu open's his eyes.. ask's
Ashu: why couldn't i see anything...
What happened!!
(Sarah hold's Ashu closely)....
Sarah: while hugging:
No issue's dear,
It's quite normal you took alot of tension.
may be we will try again some other time...
( Sarah look's at the watch.. It is 7.30 PM)
Sarah: you please relax. Will you have coffee.???
Ashu: yes i will.... ( He's still thinking)
Sarah.. ok i will get some coffee. You just relax.
(As Sarah leave's to her kitchen)...
(Ashu who is still thinking. Pick's up a chart paper.
Pick's up a pencil and he start's sketching what he saw last Night)..
First he sketches the train...
Then he sketches a platform where it's written
On the display board M..
M is the only Alphabet which is visible
and it is in yellow color..
Then on another paper he sketches

station master who is standing with lantern,
and with green flag.
In mean time Sarah get's the coffee..
She doesn't say anything...
She keep's the coffee there.
(And then she start's looking at
What Ashu was sketching...
It's becoming more darker at night and,
also heavy litghtning start's to happen...
We could hear thundering)...
Ashu start's sketching the farm house..
Sarah is noticing everything.
(Its 12.30 AM now Ashu is still sketching,
Now he sketches the name plate)..
With the name Ranjit Thakur number 603..
Now we show Ashu face is getting red,
(It seem's he's in pain. But he is not stopping.
Sarah also is not stopping Ashu).
Now he sketches the room.
Since this entire incident he saw
Was out of focus. So He sketches the room
Exactly the way he saw.
Now he sketches a out of focus lady's photo.
He also sketches the boy now...
(which is also out of focus),
Sarah pick's up both the sketches..
Ashu is sketching the stair's..
(Then he sketches that lady and and the boy
Who were laying on the floor).
Sarah is looking at the sketches.
She is not stopping Ashu.
As she want's this entire incident's had to come on paper so that
Ashu can get rid of OCD....
Ashu pick's another paper...
(He start sketching that hand of thenman
He then sketches a Pistol..)
As he sketches the Pistol
he sketches that man's wirst...

On which there is a watch
he sketches the watch..
He also Sketched a unusual ring with a dragon over it...
(As he is sketching the final lines of the entire incident's
He is slowly coming out of this zone of trans).
He gets little tired and exhausted. Weak!!
He ease himself and start getting relaxed.
Sarah hold's him hug's him..
and start massaging his shoulder.
(Ashu close's his eyes and lay in Sarah's lap's.
They both are quite)..
Now it's getting heavy thundering outside...
Suddenly Ashu get's up and start looking at the hand sketch..
Ask's: Sarah for a magnified glass.
Sarah gives him the magnified glass..
Ashu start looking at the hand and the watch..
Then he look's at the ring...
Sarah ask's: what happened.
Ashu: this watch and this ring with dragon ,
Look's like some ancient watch and ring.
I think i know i have seen these both some where
Sarah: shocking she ask's: what?? Where!!!
Ashu: tries to remmember.
He say's....
I think i have a magazine in my room.
I have a huge collection of such magazines
As it is very helpful in Advertising feild..
Sarah: so then..
Ashu : so we need to go to my house..
Sarah: ok let's go.
(Sarah want's the truth should come out
She is really concern about Ashu now)Sarah: let's go..
Sarah clinic exterior 2 AM.

Ashu start's the bike they both leaves.

# TEN

Ashu house exterior 2.15 AM..

(Ashu Sarah reaches at Ashu's House)
Ashu park's his bike...
They both very quitely open's the door,
Ashu and Sarah directly goes up to his Room.
Ashu shut's the door switch on the light's.
And he goes toward's his book shelf,
He take's out one magazine.
Swipe's some pages.
As he lift's the other one.
Satish and Sunaina come's there..
Satish: Ashu Son what happened.???
Sunaina: arey Sarah you are back too.
What are you guy's searching.???
Ashu Sarah gets scared.
Satish notices that.
Satish: what happened ?? Is everything ok??
He ask's Sarah...
Satish: very politely Sarah what happened Dear??
(Ashu Sarah are both quite).
Satish: Come! come to the living area.
(All four come's to the living room).
Sunaina: did you guy's had dinner.
Ashu: no Mom.
Sunaina: what! ok no problem
come Sarah we wil warm the food.
There is enough..in the refrigerator...sunaina say's
(The kitchen is typical western style

so from the living room the kitchen Is seen.)..
While Sunaina and Sarah are warming the food.
Satish: so my buddy what happened.??
What's cooking( mischieviously he ask's) winks.
Sarah and Sunaina come's with the food..
Now all four are sitting on the dinning table.
Sarah: Uncle. Actually i am counsellor as you know.
Satish: that's right.. we know that!
Sarah: so i got to know Ashu is a OCD.
Sunaina: ok so!!
Sarah: i know that 99% a OCD patient can be cured
By pactising Past Life Regression...
Satish: isn't that you take a OCD patient to there past life
Sarah: yes uncle you are right.
Satish: perfect i think that's the best teqhniue one can cure
A OCD patient's.
Sunaina: so what happened then?? Casually she ask's..
Sarah look's at Ashu.. who is having food.
Satish: common Son you know i am your best friend.
You have always shared everything,
Even your top secret's with me.
Don't worry say what's the problem.?)
(By this time Sarah and Ashu had finished there dinner)...
Ashu: ok dad..so as Sarah was taking me in my past life.
I saw few thing's...
A train... A platform the name was not seen properly
As the paper's were stuck on the display.
But what i could see was only M.
Satish: M!!
Ashu: yes Dad. Then i saw station master
Standing with a lantern and signalling green
Satish: ok then!!
Ashu : then i saw a farm house.
(As he mention's farm house
Satish and Sunaina exchange look's.)
Ashu goes on saying... Then i saw a name plate
Sujit Thankur with number 603.
Here Satish and Sunaina get's shocked

What!!!!? They exchange look's.
Ashu: yes i saw the same lady and a small boy playing
And then some hand pushes them from the stair case.
The same incident which i saw if you remember when i was 7.
(Satish and Sunsina exchange look's.)
Ashu: that lady beg's this man whom she called
Ranjit Thakur. But this man shoot's the lady,
And as he is about to shoot the kid.
I hear a lady scream....
Which i couldn't see. And even i got scared a
And i got up sreaming..
Ashu: all i could see was. As Ashu is about narrate futher
Satish interrupts...
Satish: listen son. I am happy you shared all these thing's with us.
And i am glad that even Sarah is trying to help you.
But...
Sunaina: but shut nothing you will stop this right now!!
Sarah you will stop this right now. OK
She adds: you have no clue Sarah
Ashu fell ill...the last time When he saw this same dream.
We had almost lost our hope of we were loosing him.
It took doctor's 15 day's to get Ashu recover.
(Now Sunaina start's crying.).
Sunaina: We almost lost you Ashu.
(Sarah comes and consoles Sunaina).
Sunaina: we don't want to loose you again.
You have to stop all this ( and she weeps)

Sarah hold's Sunaina's hands.
Satish: yes son let's stop this for a while..
Sarah: Ashu i think uncle aunty is right.
Our exam's are also coming.
Let us just concentrate on that at the moment,
Satish/ Sunaina together says; yes Sarah is right.
Ashu: (think's and say's):
yes i think you are right Mom And dad.
Satish: you promise my son..
Ashu: yes Dad you know i will not do it again i promise,

(He Goes toward's his Mom and hug's her),
Ashu say's: Sorry Mom and Dad i gave you tension,
and i am very guilty that I made Mom cry!
Sunaina come's and hug's Ashu,
Sunaina Say's: no problem Son!!
Common it's late now and as it is gonna be raining heavily.
You guy's go up to your room..
Ashu drop Sarah in the morning. Ok!
Ashu: yes Mom.!!!
Sarah say : good night Auntyji
Ashu : good night Mom and Dad,
(he hug's them and goes toward's his room)
Ashu: enter his room along with Sarah.
Ashu,; sorry Sarah for this mess.
Sarah: don't be sorry dear !!
You are part of my liife. I am happy i am with you in every way.
( They both lay on the bed and falls asleep)
Suddendly Sarah gets up.
She realises that someone has opened the door then shut's it...
(She think's may be Uncle or Aunty.
had just come up to check weather we both are comfortable).
Suddenly a very heavy lighting flashes.
So Sarah see's that magazine kept on the table.
(She pick's up the magazine and start swaping the pages.
And she see the same wrist watch which Ashu sketched
it is of some Sujit thakur.)...
She swapes the pages further and
she is even more shocked to see that ring with the
Dragon is also there which also belonged to Sujit Thakur..
(She is about to wake up Ashu. She hear a loud voice
Which is of Satish. Very quitely she open's the door.)
And she find's that Sunaina and Satish were talking
Sunaina leave's but Satish is still standing and he
Is holding a photo frame with his left hand.).
Sarah feel's that poor Uncle Aunty is in tension after all
What happened....
She turn's around to go back to the bed.
Then She stop's!!!

her eyes widened...
as the hand posture of Satish was exactly
the same as Ashu had sketched.
Sarah turn's around to look at Satish hand again..
Now flashes of sketch and Satish hand's look's similar.
Satish notice's Sarah he ask's.
Satish: very politely: do you need anything Sarah??
Sarah: yes uncle. No nothing yes i need water.
Satish: yes please take it it's in the kitchen.
Sarah: ok uncle.
(As she is walking down the stair case.
A heavy lighting happen's and she see's a photo of Ashu
And his parents of that farm house which roughly Ashu sketched
Her eyes widen up...)
(Satish is looking at her.)
Sarah notices that passes a smile to him.
As she reaches to the Kitchen,
She is confused !
Satish: Sarah beta drink the water and please
switch of the light's
Sarah: ok uncle.!!!
Satish: good night dear!!!
Sarah: go okod night Uncle..!!!
Satish goes to his room.
Sarah after drinking water switch of the light's
and start climbing the stair's...
(She look's at the photo on the wall as
She crosses the stair's she goes toward the photo
where satish was standing. )
(She look's at the photo on the wall...
She couldn't find anything.
(Then she realises that as it is uncle aunty Are disturbed.
So let it be. She turn's around,
but her kurta get stuck in the corner of the table
she turn's around to free her kurta.
(As she is pulling her kurta the draw get's open).
And she find's a Pistol in the draw.
She look's shock she removes the Pistol.

(She is even more shocked)..
Beacuse the pistol is exactly the same how Ashu sketched..
Now she start's searching inside the draw.
All of a sudden she find's the same ring with dragon
and the same wrist watch as Ashu sketched...
(Sarah is shocked she pick's up all the
thing's and as she turn's around,
Satish and Sunaina were standing.)
Sarah get's scared.
Sarah: Uncle Auntyji.??
Satish: very angrily. So you have seen alot of thing's today,
not good.
Sunaina: we told you stop this hunt.
Satish: see we have only one son.
Sunaina: and you don't have any family.
So what is the pain of a family
how would you understand.?
(Sarah trie's to scream.)
Sunaina shut's her mouth.
Its raining very heavily now.
Sunaina Sarah have a scuffle and eventually,
Sarah fall's down from the stair's and
she become's unconscious..
Satish goes toward's Ashu's room,
open's the room and find's Ashu is fast asleep...
Satish: get me a big bag. Let's take this shit and burry her the same place.
Sunaina Satish put's Sarah in big bag drag the bag to the car...
(Satish start's the car as he start's the car a very heavy lighting fall's at
near by
house..)
Ashu get's up and don't not find Sarah there.
Ashu: call's for Sarah: Sarah Sarah
(As he is calling Sarah. ).
He hear the car start's as he look's out side the window
(He sees his father car going away. )
Ashu: where is Dad going at this time.
And where is Sarah he ask's himself.
He come's out of the room call's his Mom

Ashu: Mom Mom. Strange no one is home.
(He pick's up his phone call's Sarah number.)
But the phone was kept next to the bed.
Ashu: strange Sarah mobile is here....
(Now he call's on Sunaina phone and then Satish phone
All three phone were home only.)
Ashu start's thinking what has happened no
One is home and all three did not carry there phones...
(Ashu pick's up his jacket and take bike key's,
start's his bike and start's following his father's car.
(Car is going at very fast speed,)
Satish: i somehow did had this feeling this girl wil get some trouble.
Suniana: but luckily we got it at the right time.
Let's finish this job and let's reach home fast before Ashu get's up.
Satish: yes you are right.
(Satish drives even faster.)
Ashu is riding his bike very fast.
All of a sudden the bike get's choked up
And stop's.
He check's the fuel tank. The fuel was over.
(He turn's around he could see one truck was coming
He tries to stop the truck.)
Ashu: stop stop please.....
Truck driver see's this man on the road and stop's the truck
Truck guy: what happened babu ji
Ashu: please can you give me a lift my bike fuel got over.
Truck guy: sure babu ji step in
Ashu: thank you so much....
Truck guy: where should i drop you.
Ashu: haan where does this road goes he ask's...
Truck guy: to Ratlam station.
(Ashu get's a shock he get's the same scene in front of his eyes
That the train is going and the station which he saw with the letter
Ends with M is Ratlam. Ashu is stil in trans )..
Truck guy: babu ji babu ji
Where Shall i drop you ??
Ashu: comes back to his conciousness.
Haan drop me at Ratlam station he say's...

The truck stop's at the Ratlam Station..
It is early morning 4 AM.
It is raining heavily now.
Ashu get's down at the station.
Ashu: thank you so much bhai.
Truck driver: my pleasure babu ji..
And the driver leave's...
Ashu enter's the station. He look's left right.
Then a little far off he see's the sign board
Ratlam in yellow.
He goes toward's the sign board.
Pick's up some paper's hide the entire name.
And he see's the same M which he had seen during the regression practise.
(As he turn's around we show station master standing with a lantern)
He is holding a green signal flag too.
A super fast train passes by.
So number 2 and 3 stage's of his sketches are similar...
Station master: babu ji there is no such train before 7 AM in the morning.
What are you looking at this time...he ask's..
Ashu: nothing! Since when are you here as station master.
Sation master: since 30 year's.
Ashu: are there any farm house's near by?
Station master: yes there are 5 of them!!!
Take the lantern and follow that lane you will reach the farm houses.
Ashu: that be great for you to lend me the lantern..
Station master: but do return me in the morning.
Ashu: sure i wil do so. And Ashu leave's toward's the farm house.
(Satish Sunaina has reached inside the farm house.
They both drag's Sarah out from the trunk).
Here Ashu is coming toward's the farm house.
As Satish pull's Sarah out of the bag Sarah becomes conscious,
She screams ASHU....
(Ashu who was near by hear Sarah's voice he run's toward's the farm house.)
As he crosses the main gate he come's back to see the name plate it says
Ranjit thakur 603 . So number 4 sketch is proved.
He see a man and a women are trying to beat Sarah

he come's running and jump's over the man.
They both stumble's and fall's down on the ground ,
rolling on each other,
Ashu reaches on top of this man who is Satish.
Ashu is about to hit Satish suddenly,
Lightning happen's and Satish face is visible
Ashu: what dad you.!!
Sarah comes running hold's Ashu and say's
Sarah: your father tried to kill me.
(As Sarah is about to tell Ashu the truth Ashu gets a hallucination's
All of a sudden Ashu hear's those lady and child voices.)
Ashu fall's down and he get's up
He hold's his head beneath his leg's.
He run's toward's the room...
where the lady and the boy were playing.
He see everything with naked eye..
Ashu narrate's to Sarah: i can see the lady and the boy.
They both are playing.....it is all clear now...
( As he start narrating the scenes at the same time's
he's falling and get's up again fall's down now he is in pain)
Satish Sunaina: Ashu beta Ashu ( they both cry)
Ashu; no don't come near me.
(Ashu see it again the lady come running after the boy
and the same incident happen's)
(Someone pushes both the lady and the boy from the stair case.)
Ashu: Sarah he pushed them again....
Ashu show's the spot where they both landed.
They are here... Ashu say's.
Lady: Ranjit thakur you.
You are here again...?
She plead's:...Please forgive me..
Take everything you want but,
please leave me and my son
(Now Ashu see everything clearly. )
Ashu : Sarah now i can see everything clearly..
its some Ranjit thakur who pushed Both of them
Satish and Sunaina exchanges look's.
They are shocked.

Lady: please leave us.
Man voice who is not visible
Man: i gave you last chance but you did not listen to me.
See now i have to do this ( and that man shoot's the lady)
Ashu : man kill's the lady. Ranjit Thakur kill's the lady
(Ashu fall's down he hold's his head. He's in pain..)
Satish and Sunaina again exchange look's and
they have tears in there eyes......
Man is about to shoot the little boy.
Ashu see's the same hand posture as he sketched
Which is sketch number 5.
(He see the same watch and the ring with dragon.)
Ashu: same ring and the watch its Ranjit Thakur.
So the hand is about to kill the little boy
A scream of a lady come's from away behind this hand..
Ashu see's from the hand his vision goes toward's the face of this man.
Now it revealed.
Ashu: Sarah!!! what no no its my father. Its my father.
Satish and Sunaina are shocked to see this,
Sarah is also shocked for what she is witnessing.
Ashu : who screamed. He ask's
Slowly it seems the lady who screamed is Sunaina..
Ashu see's his mother..he's shocked
Ashu : what that's my mother who screamed.
I don't believe this!!!
Sunaina who is preganant :
Ashu: Mom is pregnant...
Sunaina: Satish hurry up we need to go to the hospital,
I think water just got broke....
Satish : what about the boy??
Sunaina: just do it after the delivery.
Satish hurries and take's Sunaina to the hospital.
Leave's the boy and dead lady there...
The little boy is crying in pain
Boy: mummy mummy
Satish Sunaina reaches to the hospital.
Satish shout's for the help.
The hospital staff rushes and take's Sunaina in the operation theatre.

Here boy is about to die.
There in the hospital doctor's are preparing for a delivery
(Here boy cries in anguish and then eventually he die's)
And there in the hospital Ashu is born...
Ashu: the little boy dies and i am born i am born.
Doctor: congratulation Mr.Satish its a baby boy.
Satish: thank you so much. Can i meet my wife.
Doctor: yes you can
Satish goe's inside the operation theater.
Greet's Sunaina he hug's Sunaina look's at the baby
They both are really happy.
Sunaina: go fast finish the work left back home.
Satish: ok i finish the work and come soon.
(Satish leave's from the hospital and reaches to the
Farm house. He goes inside the same spot
as he is about to shoot the boy
he finds the boy is already Dead.)!!!!
Ashu: boy too died. Sarah dad killed both of them
My father killed lady and her son.. and i was born
Ashu to Sarah: the boy was me or what?? The lady was my mother?
Sarah is not able to say anything...
(Satish drag's both the bodies toward's the back yard
That exactly where Ashu was standing. )
Satish dig's two hole's and burries both the bodie's inside.
As he is about the fill the holes with mud a thundering start's happening
It's raining very heavily
( It is raining at present too the Similar situation of weather.?
As he fill's the hole a huge lightning fall's on the big tree
and the entire tree catches fire.)
Satish get's scared and run's from there and reache's to the hospital.
Satish: congrat's all the parcel i just courier..
Sunaina smiles... They both cuddle's the baby...
(Ashu slowly come's back to his normal conscious...
He look's at his father and mother with disbilief,)
(Then he look's up in the sky and see that huge burnt tree.
He hold's his head in disblief.)
Ashu : Oh My God. The tree is here.
So that mean's the bodies should be beneth my feets.

Ashu run's get a spade and start's digging the ground,
Satish and Sunaina are crying now.
As Ashu dig's the ground he see's two skeleton' s there
He get's scared. And he start's crying very loudly...
Ashu : Sarah my Father kilied a lady and a boy.
My Parent's are murderers.
I don't believe this.
No don't tell me Sarah its not true.
Oh God what shall i do i cannot believe this,
Please kill me i love my Parent's.
Sarah tell me its not true. Ashu Say's
To see Ashu in pain Sarah is also crying now...
Satish: son
Ashu no don't touch me Dad...
Sunaina: please forgive me.
Ashu: Mom what to do please kill me too.
As Ashu is crying very loudly a big lightning falls on the same Tree
and one big brach break's and goes inside Satish and Sunaina.
Satish Sunaina falls on the ground..
Ashu: rushes toward's his Parent's...Mom Dad Mom Dad.
He Catches both of them. But they fals down on the ground,
Now Satish and Sunaina are laying in Ashu' s hand's
Ashu: Mom Dad!!!
Satish: good it happened. It's our sin's
Sunaina: Ashu please forgive both of us.
Sunaina to Sarah : please forgive us we were about to kill you.
Sunaina folds her hand's and she die's.
Sarah:no auntyji( Sarah cries)...
Satish: Son we are extremely sorry for whatever happened.
Yes i killed my Bhabhi Sneha.. Sujit Thakur was my elder borther
Bhai told me many a times to stop drinking and playing card's.
I had alot of debt's on my head.
I requested Bhabhi to help.
But it was my mistake for my own addiction's
I killed Bhabhi and her Son Vishal...
Ashu is crying and listening..
Satish: my real name is Ranjit Thakur.
And since you saw everything it seem's

You are Vishal from your last birth whom i killed..
So it's your re-birth. I am sorry Son!
I killed you and your Mother.
Good it happened with me and your mother
In this life. It is our deed's.
Ranjit is in pain...
Son its time to leave,
Ashu: no Dad please don't leave me.
Ranjit smile's and say's.
Ashu: cries.. No Dad don't leave me..
Ranjit: It is meant to happen Son..
But you promise Me, you wll be our Son
in every birth we take.
Ashu: no dad please don't leave me.
Ranjit fold's his hands and says sorry to Sarah.
Ranjit: sorry Sarah.. please forgive me and Sunaina
And please take care of Ashu he's really good boy
And really good Son
Love you Ashu and
(Rajit dies.)
Ashu cries very loudly.... Looking up at the sky..
Ashu: Sarah see what happened he say's....
Next day morning Ashu is giving fire to all the four bodie's.
Sarah come's close to Ashu. Hug's him.
Ashu sit's down and wear his shoe's but .
does not washe hand's.
Sarah: after wearing your shoe's
Ashu you did not washed your hand's...
Ashu : yes i did it 20 time's since morning.
Sarah: hmmm i noticed it.
Welcome back Ashu....

Endssss.

Mostly
People write Pavan With W i write with V.
W means Win..
V means Victory
I will achieve my Victory
only if you my reader's will
help me to achieve my dream by reading OCD and making it real.....

# Author's Biography

I was born in delhi now i live in mumbai.
I Alway's wanted to be associated
with the social world as an actor
So i began acting as a very young age.
Did serial's for Doordarshan...
as both my Parentsl's were a film maker's in delhi.
I have acted in 50 serials on every
T.V channel's across india.
I have also acted in 150 TVC's
I did two film's as main lead.
I was professional
R'j at radio asia USA.
Now as An Author for this book 'OCD'